LISTEN
LISTEN
LISTEN

opens the door to spiritual transformation

Publisher
Louis Foundation
Eastsound Village
Orcas Island, WA 98245

Louis Gittner

SBN 0-9605492-0-X

LISTEN LISTEN LISTEN by Louis Gittner Copyright© 1980 by The Louis Foundation All rights reserved. No part of this book reproduced in any form or by any means, except for the inclusion of brief quotations in a review, without permission in writing from the publisher.
Printed in the United States of America

First Printing, October, 1980
Second Printing, June, 1981

books by
The Louis Foundation
on Orcas Island
box 210
Eastsound, WA 98245
U.S.A.

WORDS FROM THE SOURCE
VOICE OF SILENCE
THANK YOU

Listen to the voice within you,
it speaks of truth...
Listen to the whispers of nature,
the wind sings its song,
the trees whisper ageless wisdom,
the earth nurtures you
with eternal healing...
Listen to the past, the present
and the tomorrow,
They are all one and the same
viewed from different mirrors...

Acknowledgements

Special Love and Affection to all those who donated their time so unselfishly and helped bring about the completion of this book: transcribers, editors, proof readers, typists, idea-people.

And, of course, a special acknowledgment to that Source from which it all comes and to which we all are a part, without which, there would be nothing.

CONTENTS

Acknowledgments
Introduction

PROVERB ONE
Commentary 1   Where is God...................15
Commentary 2   The Magic of Reality..............21
Commentary 3   Path of Least Resistance...........27

PROVERB TWO
Commentary 4   Beyond Balance and The small 'r' before the Big 'R'..............31
Commentary 5   The Greater Perspective............39
Commentary 6   That Which you Truly Accept Shall be Yours..................43

PROVERB THREE
Commentary 7   Giving and Sharing................55
Commentary 8   The Journey and the Search.........61
Commentary 9   Law of Justice....................67
Commentary 10   Let the Water Run.................73

PROVERB FOUR
Commentary 11   Releasing........................81
Commentary 12   The Three Magic Words............89
Commentary 13   Belief...........................93

PROVERB FIVE
Commentary 14   What is My Destiny Pattern.........99
Commentary 15   Thanks-Giving....................103
Commentary 16   Meaning and Significance.........107
Commentary 17   Gifts of the Spirit................113

PROVERB SIX
Commentary 18   Should you Have a Guru...........119
Commentary 19   Committing Suicide...............123
Commentary 20   A Potpourri......................129

PROVERB SEVEN
Commentary 21   Blindness........................135
Commentary 22   The Fear of Loving...............141
Commentary 23   Blind Faith......................147
Commentary 24   A Nickel in Your Pocket..........151

PROVERB EIGHT
Commentary 25	The Power of Choice	159
Commentary 26	Perfection	165
Commentary 27	Entering the Silence	171
Commentary 28	Children of the Rainbow	177

PROVERB NINE
Commentary 29	What Do You Want for Chirstmas	183
Commentary 30	The Nature of Reality	187
Commentary 31	Letting Go	191
Commentary 32	Pine Nuts	195

PROVERB TEN
Commentary 33	You	203
Commentary 34	Law of Balance	209
Commentary 35	Love	221
Commentary 36	Words	227

PROVERB ELEVEN
Commentary 37	God is There Also	235
Commentary 38	Motherhood	239
Commentary 39	Similarities	245
Commentary 40	Grains of Sand	251
Commentary 41	A Solid Foundation	255

PROVERB TWELVE
Commentary 42	Who's Got the Truth	261
Commentary 43	Seeing the Mountain	265
Commentary 44	Synchronization	269
Commentary 45	Blessing	275
Commentary 46	The New Year	281
Commentary 47	Proper Perspective	287
Commentary 48	Oneness	291
Commentary 49	King Solomon	299
Commentary 50	Easter	303
Commentary 51	Many Questions: One Answer	309
Commentary 52	Coloring Life	311
	Epiloque	

Introduction

Each Sunday, Louis, a sensitive and Teacher of Wisdom, delivers a lesson to those who have gathered in the Chapel of Light at the Foundation headquarters on Orcas Island, Washington. The lessons contained herein are excerpts from those Sunday teachings.

Had Louis been born two thousand years ago, he would have been referred to as a Prophet. He has command of an 'extended perception' that avails him profound spiritual insights into a world without time. His place is not of this planet, but rather, a world of harmony, beauty and profundity. He's apart from the third dimension just as we are apart from the dimensions he travels.

We all can learn from his Wisdom and someday attain the heights he has at his fingertips; the worlds we now know as imaginary, and he knows as common, will be ours. For twelve years it has been my privilege to work with this man, a Master, and to grow and benefit greatly from our association.

LISTEN LISTEN LISTEN is not an intellectual book designed to excite the mind, but a book whose purpose is to spark the Creative Awareness, the

intuition, the Force within each individual. It is designed to guide those who are searching for a 'higher path', an expansion of their own Consciousness.

You will note that there are 52 chapters, one for each week of the year. Some are timely, such as the Lessons on Easter, Love – for Valentines Day, Motherhood – for Mothers Day, What Do You Want For Christmas, The New Year, Thanks-Giving. Each lesson has a profound message.

I have been told many times, "Wisdom cannot be expressed in words, the more you use them the further you get from the Truth. They are but keys to unlock the hidden Truths, to enter your silent world of Wisdom".

May the lessons contained herein unlock the Awareness within you to make your path straight and true. It's important to make the lessons a part of yourself; to act in a manner they suggest. The new worlds I have experienced with Louis can be anyone's, anytime.

Starr Farish
Vice President
Louis Foundation

1

Someday mankind
will learn that his horizon is not
as he conceives it to be...
He will learn that the horizon is
limitless
and when man functions in a
limitless world, it is then that
every moment will be a
miracle...

Commentary 1

WHERE IS GOD

Is God up? Is God down? Or here? Where is God? In heaven? Of course, if you know the answer to that question, it is assumed that you know the answer to the question, "What is God"? If you have the answers to those two questions, then: Where is God in relation to you? Is God in your mind as a beautiful thought or fantasy? Is God in your actions? Where do you place your God concept? How important is it to you? How much a part of you is it? Do you hide this concept or is it a part of your totality? Are you like some who approach this Power on a Sunday only basis?

There is a story of a man who had led a good life. He had been a kind man in many ways. He had prayed every night, "God, I'm getting to be very, very old and soon I will be dying. Before I die I'd like to meet you and talk with you." God said, "All right, I'll see you tomorrow."

The man was happy and jumped for joy. He could not sleep that night. Tomorrow God was coming! He cleaned his house, polished the copper and laid a fire in the fireplace and made a big pot of stew with all types of marvelous vegetables and herbs. He got out the best that he could offer because, after all, God was coming!

Very early in the morning there was a knock at the door. The little man hurried to open it, and there was an old man asking for some food. He quickly asked him to leave saying, "Oh, I'm awfully sorry. Ordinarily, I would feed you but I can't today. God is coming! Go on your way!" And the man shut the door and continued his task of cleaning and getting ready for God.

After an hour or so a woman knocked at the door asking for a cup of water. Again the man shut the door, saying "Lady, I'd like to help you, but I can't today. God is coming! I must give all my efforts in preparation for Him!" During the day there were a succession of knocks on the door with people asking for similar things. Each time the door was closed.

The day progressed, the hours passed and dusk approached. The man sat in the large chair by the fireplace wondering when God was going to arrive. The time ticked by and soon it was midnight. The candles had burned out and the fire turned to embers. The man couldn't understand. He fell down on his knees and said, "God! God! You told me you were coming today, and I prepared for you. I prepared the best I had. Why did you let me down?" After a few moments of silence the answer came. "I came many times today and knocked upon your door but you wouldn't let me in."

Many people behave like the old man. Should we be conceptualizing God as something apart from us? Have we limited our concept to only a fragmentary part of God? Do we recognize God? Are we dealing with something "apart from"? Can we separate things?

In reality everything is a part of the One and God is the One. Where is God? Everywhere and nowhere. What is God? Everything and nothing. Where do you fit into this picture?

Commentary 2

THE MAGIC OF REALITY

ouldn't it be wonderful to be able to go to a store and purchase magic things? You could have all sorts of pleasures. And yet, in one perspective, everything is magic only we don't look upon it in that way. Magic deals with illusion.

As we grow older we lose our sense of wonder. Consequently, we become what some would title sophisticated. With sophistication comes boredom, and with boredom comes all the sticky, unpleasant ramifications that life can hold. With the world of Wonder, it's different. It's a world of expectation, a world of anticipation, a world of Joy.

Ponder a small action such as a plant growing and the processes it goes through. If you have ever seen

a speeded-action film of the growth of a plant, you will have noticed that fantastic things are involved. The plant stretches, weaves, gyrates. First it is a seed, then a plant, a bud, and suddenly a flower or fruit. When you think that this great burst of life comes from a tiny seed, sometimes so small you can hardly see it, isn't this magic?

We get involved with the unimportant things. There's a tendency to spend much time worrying, fretting, and frowning. We restrict the Joy from coming into our lives. It is because we are concerned with the outside things that we don't spend enough time with the inner experience. We don't take time to listen, to feel, to touch, to smell, to see, to experience in a total sense. Yet if we would do so, there would be no room for boredom.

It has been written that laughter is good for the soul, and this is a true statement. Not a phoney social laugh but a good-hearted belly laugh. When you are laughing, you are joyous, you are filled with wonder, you are receptive only to the finest and most uplifting vibrations. You will find it difficult to laugh and have negative thoughts.

Regard every minute, every day with wonder. Expect magical things and you will see them performed. Your world will be filled with the magic of the True Reality.

Commentary 3

PATH OF LEAST RESISTANCE

The path of least resistance produces little or no growth. The pond that goes nowhere or does nothing is polluted. The running brook does not have time to become polluted. In directed or structured movement, there is achievement, growth. Let the wind, stars and babbling brook teach you the rhythm of life.

2

Love builds highways
out of dead ends...

Commentary 4
BEYOND BALANCE AND THE SMALL 'r' BEFORE THE BIG 'R'

LESSON ONE: Go Beyond Balance.

Many people talk in terms of achieving balance: Going from chaos or an unorganized pattern on some level to harmony, organization and order on another level.

But balance is not a growing thing. It is a hiatus. It's all right to want to reach a balance and get your "head on straight," but this is not enough. To reach this plateau is one thing, to go beyond it is another. We come to the earth plane to grow and you cannot grow by remaining on a plateau. It must be used as a springboard to greater heights. Action is the key.

It is important to create a good life, but the true secret is to have a good life LIVED. It is

good to arrive at a point of harmony in your life and a place of stability, but after you arrive at that point, you must go beyond it into a growing situation. Some people stop there and that is a mistake. You don't stop until you get to the top of a mountain and you will find when you get to the top there is always another mountain beyond. It is a continuous process. So don't stop at any one point, keep going. You do need the plateaus, they are good, but don't look upon them as the ultimate.

LESSON TWO: You Must Understand the Small 'r' Before You Can Understand the Big 'R'.

There are many thousands of people who receive our lessons each month. One day Mrs. Smith read a lesson and thought, "These lessons are very good. I like them." Then she saw that it was signed by a man named Louis. "I wonder what he looks like?" So Mrs. Smith projects a Louis. "He must look like Jesus." He must be good looking and have big brown eyes. He must also be skinny and young and all the things that we think are admirable traits today.

Then Mrs. Smith meets Louis. Here is a man who is overweight and not young, he has brown eyes but he doesn't look like her fantasy. What does Mrs. Smith do? She feels betrayed, her image is shattered. She'll never again be able to take seriously the monthly lesson. She couldn't handle the small 'r' (reality) and so she couldn't go beyond it to the Big 'R' (Reality).

Diamond rings may come out of tin cans. The container doesn't change the beauty of the jewel. You must comprehend 'reality' before you can comprehend 'Reality.' You must understand this dimension before you can understand other dimensions. You have to be able to handle one dimension before you can handle another dimension. How can you expect to understand the spiritual realm before you understand the physical realm?

Accept reality. Accept things as they are, not as you think they should be or as you fantasize them to be. Everything is as it is and it is as it should be. All things on the physical level are moving towards perfection.

Everything on the spiritual level is in a state of Perfection. Your job is to realize that Perfection. That is the secret: Perfection is everywhere. Everything is already God. Everything is in order, but you must realize it.

You can realize self. And when you understand self you can understand everything because you are part of the Universe, part of the Cosmos. If you understand one drop of water, you can understand the ocean, and as you understand the small 'r' you can go on and comprehend the Big 'R'.

Commentary 5

THE GREATER PERSPECTIVE

Often in my meditations I reflect back to conversations Leon, my teacher, and I shared. I remember Leon talking one day about fragmented living, fragmented awareness, fragmented consciousness. He often referred to life as a jigsaw puzzle. Part of the fun or joy of living lies in finding one piece that fits together with another piece until the picture is whole. But, warned Leon, don't be concerned if the first few pieces come together to make a jackass. That doesn't mean the whole puzzle will be of jackasses.

It's apparent that you must have the pieces to make the whole, but it's also apparent that once you have the whole, it may not be understood. In ten minutes you know more about something than you do in one minute, in ten days you know even more, and

in ten weeks, still more. Some day you will be able to comprehend it fully.

When you take little bits and pieces of a puzzle and put them together to make a picture do not get caught up with each isolated piece. Think in terms of the whole rather than in terms of the parts. True, parts make the whole, but not all parts are alike. Not all parts have the same shape, the same color, or the same vibrational intensity. It's important to be aware of the parts and to understand them, and to know that they are wholes unto themselves. But you must wait until you can look at many pieces before you comprehend the bigger whole.

Strive for a continuum, a time for putting things together and a time for looking at things from a greater perspective. Once the whole is understood, then you can act in accordance with it, with Wisdom.

Commentary 6

THAT WHICH YOU TRULY ACCEPT SHALL BE YOURS

here are certain universal laws that govern our existence and whether we are aware of them or not does not really matter, they govern anyway. As you expand your consciousness and become aware of some of these principles, you have a divine obligation to do your best and to act in accordance with them. Man-made laws may be bent, twisted, distorted. With spiritual law, there is no bending, no evading. They Are.

One such cosmic law is "That which you truly accept shall be yours." Now, there are many ways of stating this principle, but the law is the law, regardless. Let us examine it closely: That which we accept, that which we truly accept, shall be ours. What do we mean by "truly accept?" Let's look at this on a very human level.

Some years ago in Phoenix, Arizona, a daily newspaper reported mass robberies. Several days in a row the headlines were the same: Robberies. One particular block seemed to be harder hit than the others. There was a lady who became very affected by the newspaper headlines and she installed locks on all her doors because she knew there was going to be a robbery. It had to be! She had accepted it. Robberies occurred daily and she employed all of the latest defensive devices. There were burglar alarms of all types, watch dogs, special police. Nevertheless, the woman's house was robbed. She had accepted it, it was hers. There was another older woman on the same block whose house was not broken into. She was a love-giver and she knew she would have no problems. She didn't. She Blessed her house, surrounded it in Light. She put forth a strong 'force-field' of protection.

The way this law works is interesting. Take the case of the common cold. When a person says, "I think I have a cold," that's the first step. It is in the mental processes. Then because we think we have a cold, we start feeling it. It takes a larger form. The symptoms, whether they were there or not, will be forthcoming shortly: headache, fever, sore throat,

sniffles. First, is the process of thinking you have a cold, then of feeling that you have a cold, of producing the "stage effects," and then to share it with people. This can be a very subtle, even unconscious act. Of course, we have to tell the world about it because it's nice to have sympathy. "I have a cold." We label it and a label is a strange thing. It can be very destructive because once you have pronounced a cold to the world, you have given it life. Your sympathetic friend will act as an echo and say, "Yes, you have a cold, that's too bad."

How many times has this happened? It happens all the time. How about the person who says, "I know, I won't be successful, I know I won't get the job." By putting energy and form into something like this, of course it is exactly what will happen. That person won't be successful, will he? How many times have you heard, "I expected this to happen. I knew it was going to happen!" It did. That which you truly accept will be yours.

Sometimes we're like a fish at the bottom of the sea. We open our mouths and gullibly accept. We can be caught by the hook, can't we? When we're on line, it's difficult to get rid of it.

You need to examine your thoughts. You need to examine your words. You need to examine your actions. If life is not going as you desire, and if you want to change it, then do some exploring. You will find if you go to the basis of what you have, you have accepted all that you have on one level or another.

One of the first women doctors of medicine in the southwest, a very powerful person, was a lady by the name of Christine. She lived by the Truth. She talked to me about a great epidemic when she was administering to thousands of people. People thought that she would surely become infected. But she knew she wouldn't. She did not accept it. She knew, "I had a job to do and the sickness was not going to knock on my door." She administered to the sick all through the epidemic, and she did not become ill. Had she once thought "My goodness, all these other people have it, I will have it, too.", she would have given it form. It would have been hers.

Think of how many times this principle affects your life. Do you get up in the morning and say, "This is going to be a crummy day, a lousy day," and, sure enough, it is. Of course, you can blame it on all sorts

of things. You can say it's because of the weather, because of other people or other circumstances. But, in actuality, it is none of these things. It is you who proclaimed it, who brought it into manifestation. Frequently, there is acceptance, proclamation, labeling. If you want tears and sorrow, just think how sad you are and they will flow.

The power called God can be used in many ways. It can be likened to electricity. We can take that energy and do marvelous things with it; put light where there is no light, run motors in machines, or end a life. It's a form of the same power. And, so it is with acceptance. You can accept that which is beautiful, that which is worthy of you, or you can accept that which is unworthy. It's all up to you.

3

Cast your bread upon the water
and it comes back sandwiches...

Commentary 7

GIVING AND SHARING

Recipients of mail frequently are asked to give to a charity. It is a word that is used so often that it is abused. The concept of giving has been warped and put on the level of dollars and cents: Give your dollars; Send your checks. Cosmically, it's much more than this. Giving can be on many levels, and on the highest level this action is no longer giving, it becomes a thing called Sharing.

When you donate to an organization you may have no idea how it will be used, the process is very impersonal. With a pristine form of giving – Sharing – there is a personal involvement. When you share something, an elevation takes place, a raising of consciousness. Everything that is involved in a Sharing is lifted on a vibratory level.

This is the lesson in the story of the loaves and fishes. This is the lesson that is given many times in the Bible, the expression of the Unity of the Divine Mind. If you have bread and break it in half and share it with someone else, suddenly that bread becomes a sacrament and your life becomes a part of that sacrament. As with the brightening of the lamps in a dining room when the wick is turned up there is an adding to, a becoming more of, a glorifying, for we are truly a part of everything that we do. When you share a smile, a glance with someone, a touch, this becomes a moment in which consciousness is elevated and there is awareness of the Oneness with all things for that is a part of the sharing process.

Nothing really belongs to you. No one owns anything. You have things in your stewardship, things that you have for the moment, but those in essence do not belong to you. You may use them, true. But, if you just use a thing, it becomes mundane, its significance remains within the three dimensions. When you take that thing and Share it, it takes on a different vibration, it is elevated to the plane of true significance. Go back to the piece of bread: you have a little loaf and you sit down and

eat it, an insignificant event, a small thing, a piece of food.

But break that bread with someone, Share it, and there is awareness of a higher concept, of entering into the Eternal Reality of things. People talk about the raising of consciousnes, of entering higher levels of being. This is a process. Sharing is the key.

Commentary 8

THE JOURNEY AND THE SEARCH

In this process of living on this earth, there is a beginning and an end. From the cosmic point of view, the beginnings are part of the endings and the endings are part of the beginnings. It is a continuum. We enter into various experiences called "living": we might have one experience in Russia, the next in Spain, and so on. Sometimes, an individual will stay in one area of the world for a long period of time. We find, also, in this continuum of experiencing and growing, that we take on different bodies. We might have a female body one time and a male body the next. We might be black or another color. This, though it adds some flavor to the continuum, is insignificant by itself. The significance lies in what is done in a particular body in a particular place and time, and in the reason behind the "why."

If you were to look at life as a journey, a search, maybe that would give it direction and meaning. What is the journey and what is the search? Where is the roadmap? You bring the map with you but many times it is lost or forgotten or you haven't bothered to look at it to see what is to be accomplished.

What do I have to do? Where are my shortcomings? How can I serve? What about the direction? There is direction in one's life, but where does it come from? It comes from the silence, by entering into a time of being still and knowing. This is where direction comes from, not by running and looking here and there, but by closing your eyes and going within. Here we find a gentle nudging, not "Now do this, now do that," but a nudging. The more you listen to this inward direction and the more you follow it, the clearer it becomes and the more direction you'll have.

It is easy to get distracted from the road, to be involved in all kinds of diversions. Many fall madly in love with themselves and get caught up in the "I" – "I did this and I did that," and "I" can get to be very much of a stumbling block. But, if you really examine the situation, "I" did nothing. It is the "Father that worketh through you." Some get

caught up in concepts like "I must make a lot of money" or other whimsies. In the silence, you will be nudged towards getting on with the show! Getting on with the job!

Is there a goal? The goal might be called self-realization, self fulfillment, at-one-ment, realizing who and what you are and acting in accordance with it.

Where do you go and whom do you look to? It doesn't matter. The key is what you do where you are. You have chosen this time and this place for growth. What are you doing about it?

Is there One Answer to all this? It's easiest to see it in Nature. There you will find balance, harmony, beauty, giving.

The answer lies in yourself if you will look within. These will not be intellectual answers with labels. Rather, intuitive answers with nudgings. But there is only One Answer and One God, and that answer lies in the realm of the creative power and directing force of the universe. Go within and you will find it. The journey and the search may be one.

Commentary 9

LAW OF JUSTICE

he Law of Justice is a subject that is difficult to accept because it infers that everything is in order, you are getting exactly what you deserve; no more, no less. There are no exceptions. There are no accidents. Everything is in balance. On the third dimensional level, it can be equated thusly: You're fat because you eat too much; You have a miserable life because of the words, thoughts and actions you project; You're poor because you know you can't be a success.

On a higher level: You are where you are because you have lived in accordance with universal law to the extent that it puts you there.

There comes into everyone's life things that aren't liked. Usually, the blame is put somewhere else. If we are very orthodox we might blame the Devil —

he caused it. Other times the "they" can become a good thing to blame. Seldom is it I or we. But if we were spiritually mature, we would look to where the seed atom is planted. If we look closely, we see that it is planted within us.

Life is like a garden. If we don't bother to plant it, there's going to be a random crop of weeds. If only onions are planted, then only onions will grow. If you want your life to be a beautiful and harmonious one, then plant such a life in the universe by seeding it with your thoughts and actions. Put forth as you want your harvest to return.

When someone says, "No one loves me." I ask them, "Whom do you love"? Love must be sent forth for love to come to you. You don't have to run here and there looking for it, you can find it right where you are. This law applies to any facet of your life.

Everything has a price, the breath you take, everything you do, every moment. This is why tithing is important. But there are many types of tithes; money, energy, time. The dollar placed in the collection plate at church means very little. How much of your life are you Sharing with others? How much energy and action? Everything is recorded, as

if by a big computer, and everything that you give forth comes back. True, it might not return in a day or a month or a year. But, sometime, in one form or another, it will come back. And, you have control over what comes back to you.

How can you have the kind of life that is happy and good? By projecting that life, putting it into action, planting your garden with positive things and taking care of the growing plants.

This is a kingdom of God, you have your being in God, and everything that comes into your life has a reason, purpose. Within your being, within the universe, are all the answers, the causes, everything. Within you there is a flame of the True God or Universal Consciousness burning brightly. A part of your job in being here is to make it burn more brightly. Act in accordance with this Law. Project. Receive. You are the winner.

Commentary 10

LET THE WATER RUN

There is a new wave of awareness, a new mass consciousness labeled the "I" generation consciousness. This infers a generation which is basically concerned about one thing; themselves. As a part of this newness, people don't want to get married, they don't want the commitment. People don't want to have children because it interferes with what they'd like to do. There is emphasis on 'my space,' 'my thing!' Even dancing is solo.

Most of the modern self-help programs are psychologically oriented with the emphasis on the individual. While it's good to love yourself, respect yourself, be proud of yourself, it's not good to get to a point where you eat, sleep and live for yourself. It's then that something starts breaking down in the fiber of mankind. Mankind is like a piece of cloth,

composed of many threads. You and I, we're all one of those threads. If they are not interwoven into a harmonious pattern, then, instead of a piece of cloth, we have nothing but a bunch of threads.

To graduate to a greater level of understanding you must realize the value of Serving. It is one of the hardest concepts for people to grasp, primarily because there is such great emphasis on the self, the I. Whom do you think about mostly; whom do you talk about mostly? If you find it's yourself, then your situation is out of balance and, in time, it can become a negative destructive force.

You cannot grow by focusing your energy on yourself. It must be focused on a greater perspective.

Energy can be likened to water. If water flows, it is fresh, sparkling, vibrant water. But, if it sits in a pool and is contained, then it becomes stagnant. The same with energy. It must flow and keep flowing. This is what service does. It promotes the flow, it increases the flow. You, through service, act as a channel for the energy to flow through for the benefit of all. This unselfish act benefits everyone and, in turn, benefits you.

You're living in a very exciting, accelerated time. In the days ahead you're going to see many changes in the way we live. You're going to see the end of many types of diseases. There will be changes and advancement in technology.

You must advance, too. You are not to stagnate. You are to Share, Serve, Grow and 'let the water run freely.'

4

Labels are not all that important,
they are but fleeting shadows...

Commentary 11

RELEASING

One of the big problems in growing is perfecting the process of releasing. It is too easy to remain where we are and to protect what we have. We're closed to something new because we're afraid of it. We're not sure we can handle it. We may be in a miserable rut and not like it or the conditions that surround it but at least we're familiar with it. There's an old Chinese legend: One day God said, "You all feel heavily burdened, so on a day and at a place that I will pick, you are to unload these burdens. But when you do, you must take another with you." The people thought, "Oh, isn't this marvelous! We can unload our problems, all our worries!" And they went to the appointed place and gleefully put down their burdens and took another upon them. But in a few days they came to God and said, "Let us have our old troubles back. At least we were comfortable with them. We knew those

burdens. The new burdens we can't understand. They're much heavier than those we gave up."

It is questionable whether we really want to unload our burdens. We say we do, but the only way to unload a burden is to release it, let it go, to be free, open, unobstructed. Yet, with all the talk about being a free person in a country dedicated to freedom, is this what is really wanted?

With freedom comes responsibility. That is the burden you acquire as you release the old burdens. It is a spiritual responsibility and because this is something that has not yet been experienced, there's a fear. It's difficult to let go. If you would open up your thinking, your doing, reconstruct your patterns, many things would open to you. If you would but open the door, the mind, the heart, "Let go and let God," all things would be available to you.

As long as you have desires, as long as you have to have things, you will not get to know God fully. When you get to the point where you can release and be desireless then you have reached the point where you can know God. The question is, where

do you place your God? What is important to you, the search for Meaning or the search for things? Will you go inward or do you go outward?

As long as you go outward, you'll only "know about," but when you go inward you are going to "Know." But you can't turn within if you don't first let go; you can't turn within if you are pulling a cartload of desires behind you. These desires are going to make barriers, they are going to impede you. The desiring of things is a false, shallow desire. As you reach the essence within yourself, you'll find that your true desire has always been what is truly to Know, to be at one with God. There are only a few people who know God, totally. You must open your heart and be full of Love. If the heart is full of Love, there is no room left for the alienating powers of hatred, or fear, or greed, or the burdens that restrain the full expression of Love. Open doors; open minds; open hearts; never, never close them.

If you want a revelation today, look up the word desire in your dictionary. Then release, let go, Be. God is so much more than you imagine. Open All To Him.

There is a poem called "Memo" that has profound implications. It may trigger or inspire you to greater heights. Ponder it, become it. Share this "Memo" with others:

> Please open doors, don't close them;
> Open minds, keep them open;
> Open hearts, never, never close them;
> God is so much more than you imagine,
> God is so much more than we imagine,
>   Open all to Him.
>   Author Unknown

Commentary 12

THE THREE MAGIC WORDS

In U. S. Anderson's book, THREE MAGIC WORDS, the author says he's going to give you the secret of all life. After you read through the book you finally come to the last page and he gives you the magic words: YOU ARE GOD. If I spoke these magical words to most metaphysicians they would agree. But, I don't think any of us know that we are God because knowing means having an understanding totally from the ends of our toes to the tops of our heads, whether we are driving the car or washing our clothes, or playing the violin. This understanding has not become a part of very many people. Perhaps we should be as children and sit down and write it a thousand times, or do as some people do, make placards and put them in many places so that when they're shaving or brushing their teeth they are constantly being reminded.

The lack of Knowing is a shortcoming. Most people only know-about, they don't really Know. They have a surface understanding that they are God and a part thereof but still they are concerned with the "I'm not perfect" aspect. This assumes a separation from the functioning of the Divine Mind. It is this concept of separation that is the most troublesome to overcome. To do so, the student must Know that God has no boundaries, God is All, God is Perfection, and everything is in the process of manifesting this Perfection of Being within itself. There is a concept called falling from Grace. This is falling from a True understanding of what we are and acting like it; a falling into a limitation of our own making where we forge the feelings of unworthiness, narrowness, lifelessness. "Who, little me?" To come into a realization of the energetic truth is the task at hand.

> Everything Is God;
> I Am God;
> You Are God;
> We Are God.

It's time to start acting like it!

Commentary 13

BELIEF

round the world human beings hold different concepts of life. Americans were appalled a few years ago when Asian Monks poured gasoline on themselves and ignited it. It was their belief that it was the right thing to do. Belief is a way of life, a thing of action, just as Love is a thing of action.

You need not die for your beliefs. Rather, it is something to live for, something that makes life valuable, worthwhile. Many people interpret belief only as a verbal thing, something just to be talked about. They say, "This I believe, these things I hold 'True' but their actions go contrary to their words. They find themselves going in two directions at once: their words saying one thing, their actions saying another. When this occurs, and it happens to

everyone at some time, they find themselves confused and unhappy because they can walk only one path. "A house divided will fall"; a man divided will fall as well. One of the purposes of coming into this expression of consciousness called Life is to become whole, to become One, to become "total," to become synchronized. When your life glorifies your belief or expounds or expresses it, not only in words but in actions, then you are reaching your totality.

There comes a time in each of our lives when we must examine our beliefs honestly and directly, without side stepping, and we must look at what we are doing about them. What do you believe in? You should believe in everything. This does not sidestep the issue because God is everything, manifested and unmanifested. You are everything, manifested and unmanifested, as well. Believe this, and act accordingly.

5

The man who puts the
most wood on the fire gets
the warmest blaze...

Commentary 14

WHAT IS MY DESTINY PATTERN

What is the purpose of life? It is to fulfill your destiny pattern. Everyone's destiny is basically the same, to Love and to Give. This may be too simple for most people, but it's true. To Love and to Give may be approached by each individual differently. Each person has different attributes with which to attain this end and each is a unique unit, but the overall goal is the same: to Love and to Give.

To Love doesn't refer to Valentine's Day, a card and some candy. Giving is not donating ten dollars to a charity. Both refer to a way of life, Loving and Giving in its truest sense. They are verbs, action, a way of approaching all things. They are attitudes. You come to add to, you come to make life. You did not come to hate and take.

Ask yourself, "Am I loving and am I giving"? If the answer is no, then do something about it. If the answer is yes, then say to yourself: "How can I do more"?

Commentary 15

THANKS-GIVING

While in a large metropolitan city, I recently overheard two bedraggled old men sitting on a bench, imbibing and discussing Thanksgiving. "What do we have to be thankful for? Riots, hippies, drugs, poverty. Why do we have Thanksgiving"?

The word Thanksgiving is composed of two different parts: Thanks-Giving. What these two gentlemen were really saying, is Thanks Taking. They had missed the point. The point is to give thanks, to set forth in motion a giving of thanks. In order to do this it is not necessary to have an object to be thankful for like a turkey on the table. Rather, it is like sowing seeds. When you start sowing seeds of thanksgiving into the cosmos, you are preparing for a harvest. When you give thanks you prime the pump, you start the flow.

All things respond to and are part of the Divine Flow. This is a Cosmic principle. If we adhere to this principle, things go well. If we disregard the principle, we are subject to many challenges in life. Things don't go right.

Don't forget the spiritual aspect of this holiday. Don't get caught up in the reaping, the taking, and forget the Giving of Thanks. Don't forget your life within the Great Flow, within the Life that is everywhere Divine, the Life of which you can become conscious if you will but open to it. Give thanks wherever you are just for being a part of this Divinement.

Commentary 16

MEANING & SIGNIFICANCE

With building and construction, there comes a restructuring of the contour of the land. Recently, I witnessed a lilac that was uprooted and died during this process and I couldn't help but feel sad. For many years the plant tried to fulfill its destiny pattern; it struggled. The soil was very poor, but the plant existed and witnessed many changes. The plant had meaning, significance. All life is precious.

If nothing had value to us, life would be hollow and there would be no beauty. There would be little reason to continue. Everything that you see and experience and feel and know is a reflection of you. If you see beauty, that beauty begins within you. If you find significance in something, it begins within you. It represents a level of awareness.

Stones appear to have no meaning other than they are stones. From one viewpoint, they are insignificant objects. From another point of view they can have tremendous importance. Wars have been fought and people have died over valued stones. In some cultures, they have been revered as having high religious significance, as being talismans, as having curative powers. Is the stone valuable or is it what man attributes to the stone that gives it significance? Is it because the rock you pick up on the beach has no price tag that it can be tossed aside?

In the three dimensional sense there are no inherent meanings, no set values. You are able to make your own valuations. In one country a tree may be regarded as sacred, in another, the same tree may be chopped down for kindling. But as you go on to other dimensions, meaning starts to take on a different context because it goes out of the realm of emotion, out of the realm of the qualities that are human. It goes into the realm of Structure, into the realm of Meaning and Significance. As you extend your Awareness you enter the realm of Cosmic Order where the Laws are constant and hold the universe in a harmonious balance. Extend your awareness to the Ultimate, and you will reach that

level, or matrix, where all is one. The "place" is the Truth, or God.

Meaning and significance depend upon what chords are struck within you upon your level of consciouness or upon where you are.

Thank you, little lilac, for the lesson.

Commentary 17

GIFTS OF THE SPIRIT

THE GIFT OF TOUCH — What a beautiful gift that is! To be able to reach out and touch, not only physically but on other levels. With touching comes feeling, communication, the blending of personalities, vibrations. What a beautiful, beautiful gift.

THE GIFT OF SIGHT — Many people think of the gift of sight as looking rather than seeing, but these are two different things. What a wonderful gift it is to be aware of all the beauty around us, to be aware of the aspects of God that are all about, the miracles that are taking place every moment. Little miracles. Big miracles. Some you can comprehend and some you can't. You'll find that sometimes you can touch more with your hands in your pockets and you can see more with your eyes closed. Learn to touch and see with your heart.

THE GIFT OF LISTENING – Think of all the things we can hear. Listen to a bird. Isn't the song that bird sings beautiful! There are so many things to be aware of through listening; the music of a child's laughter, the sounds beyond the Silence. These lovely gifts come to us.

THE GIFT OF LOVING – What a gift it is to be able to love and be loved. What a wonderful gift to love in any way that you can. There are many, many levels of loving. Love may be equated to a brass band or a violin. Sometimes loving is very quiet and has no sound at all. What a beautiful gift it is.

Are you using your gifts? They're very special. Are you using them to their utmost? It seems we abuse them rather than use them. All these lovely gifts are ours and the greatest of them all is the gift of life.

Use your gifts in the traditional sense and then transcend with them into the realm of feeling. To really feel with your gifts is a great lift of the Spirit.

6

Thoughts without actions
are burdens, but once the action
takes place, they are lifted
beyond the burden...

Commentary 18

SHOULD YOU HAVE A GURU

No one has a corner on Spirituality or Consciousness. Each person comes equipped with the "all." The question is how to get in touch with or to recognize this totality. Sometimes a guru helps. Not that a guru can give you a magic formula to inward awareness, but that some people need this help, others don't. It can quicken the path or it can be a hindrance.

For me, a teacher was necessary. I came to this lifetime with all the pieces in my consciousness but I was unable to accurately formulate the picture. I saw auras, knew about life and death, perceived the structure of the universe, but I didn't know how it all related. Leon helped. He was very wise. He helped me, he didn't do for me. He was aware of the many dimensions, their meanings and how they all fit together.

There are very few like him. I was blessed to be one of his pupils.

He had a structure for teaching. One was, that in a day's time, there could only be 12 questions. If there were more than 12 questions, they would have to wait for another day. If I had a question, I was required to wait 15 or 20 minutes before I asked it to see if it really was a question. I couldn't just pop out with any old question that came bouncing into my consciousness. Sometimes, I already knew the answers to the questions I asked Leon. I needed confirmation. I needed fortifying.

Some people see gurus as objects. It is something that will take them somewhere. Many people trade in gurus like cars. It was my understanding from Leon that you're allowed only one in a lifetime. It is not a relationship to be treated lightly.

So, does one need a guru? Some people do, some don't. Only if you think you do. It may depend on how high you want to travel.

Commentary 19

COMMITTING SUICIDE

 recommend that everyone commit suicide, not in the usual sense of killing, but in the sense of killing or changing what you now are into what you can be. This transitional process is performed through the act of Love. It's the act of letting go of what you think you are and becoming what you really are. That is a type of suicide. You might call it a rebirth. It has many names.

This process called growing is a matter of change. It's the one constant we have in this world. There's a continual change going on in your body: cells being replaced, new hair and new skin, a new everything every seven years. But growing can change not only on the physical level, but on the nonphysical level as well - a letting go of some of your old ideas, your old approaches to things. It is

accomplished not as a word, not as a concept, but as a way of life. It is then that it takes on significance and purpose.

This small speck in the universe we call Earth is changing daily. People are gathering together to study, meditate, and act, to commit suicide and emerge with a new self. They are letting go of their old patterns and they are growing and expanding within. This is occurring on all continents. It's a very exciting time to be on the earth.

With change or suicide, there'll be some growing pains. Just as puberty brought physical and emotional problems, so also will building a "new you" bring growing pains. It is a type of spiritual puberty, if you will. It's very difficult to let go of old patterns. If you're in a rut and don't like it, you can still cope with it. You don't know if you'll like a new you or what it will be like. After all, a new pair of shoes can give you blisters. The new ones might be better shoes, more up-to-date, but the old won't give you blisters.

To grow might also blister your ego. You will have to give and let go. But, when you let go and "Let

God," something happens. Something within you expresses itself. It is time right now, not tomorrow, not the next day, to begin. It is time right now to commit yourself to what you really are, to be that beautiful person you can be. Think of who you are and where you are and what is occurring around you and what you are a part of. You are alive in the most exciting time in history. Rockets are going into the air and people are going down into the earth. Others are finding rocks on the moon and algae on the bottom of the sea. But, the people who are making an inner exploration are finding specimens that don't even have names, fascinating and beautiful things that were utterly unknown to them. These people are, in a joyous sense, committing suicide, letting go of who they thought they were and discovering who they really are. And in discovering this, they are making, at long last, the acquaintance of Love.

Commentary 20

A POTPOURRI

A DIFFERENT APPROACH:

Two priests were discussing the monies of their respective churches. They were talking about how the donations came in, what to spend them on, etc. The Catholic Priest said, "Well, I take the money that comes in and I count it. I divide it in half and say, this half is for you, God, and this half is for me. That seems fair and square." The Rabbi said, "Well, I have a different way of doing it. I take all the money and throw it up in the air and say, 'God, catch all you can.' What falls to the ground, I keep."

It's a matter of how you approach things, isn't it? Neither is good or bad, just a different approach.

CYCLES:

There are four seasons in the year: Summer, Fall, Winter, Spring. Be aware of the seasons because what is going on outside you is also a part of what is going on inside you. There are changes in the rhythms of nature and when they change, you change. Observe these changes and work with them. To be aware is to recognize what is happening and to work and flow with it. This is also one way you can grow and expand your consciousness.

LABELING:

"Labels are for pickle jars, not for human beings." Often labels stem from ignorance and to categorize by labeling is to limit something to our own restricted perspective. They may be unjust or cruel or meanings may be conveyed that were not meant to be. They may also leave a great deal to the imagination. Everyone's seen a circus poster that portrays the circus in one picture. Labels tend to do this and avoid the far more intricate picture. So, as you go about your life, remember: "Labels are for pickle jars and not for human beings."

7

I am limited only to the limits
I place upon myself and others...

Commentary 21

BLINDNESS

nce upon a time, many years ago, there was a wise teacher who had four pupils. The four pupils had one thing in common: they were blind. In a conversation one day, the teacher spoke to them of elephants. "But, Master," said one of the students, "we don't understand. What is an elephant?" The wise teacher answered, "If you want to truly know what an elephant is, you must find out for yourself."

So the four blind men went on a journey. They went to a place where there were elephants and asked of the owner. "Show us an elephant." "All right," he said, "here is an elephant." And each of the four students examined the animal in his own way. One of the students was led to the trunk; he felt the trunk and said to himself, "Aha!" Another student examined the tail; he reached out and soon said,

"Aha!" The third felt the foot, and the fourth examined yet another portion of the animal.

The students returned to the teacher and said, "We know what an elephant is now." He said, "Oh, do you?" "Yes," said one, "it's a long tube" and he gave a very apt description of the trunk of the elephant. Another student said, "Oh, no, it's hairy and it wiggles." He described the tail. The other two pupils spoke of the parts of the animal they had examined. Each of them felt sure that he now knew what an elephant was; each had experienced it.

If you really get the point of this story you know that the blind students represent mankind today. Too often a particular aspect of a situation is examined, understood, and thought to accurately reflect the composition of a much larger picture. What you want to develop is 360 degree sight, to be able to see all around a situation and to understand it from many viewpoints. You need to examine and re-examine your impressions, your reactions, your feelings, until you know that you are not looking at just a part of or from an obstructed viewpoint. Narrow-mindedness knows one point of view and that's it. How easy it is to make assumptions on very fragmented evidence or even on hearsay. "Well, he

told me" or "she heard him say." This may be distorting. To think you understand in this manner results in blindness.

Examine that with which you are involved more carefully and extensively. Use your hands, your ears, your eyes. But, more importantly, examine it with your heart, your intuition. Examine first intellectually until you fully comprehend on that level and then use your inner resources so you can understand it even further. You will discover that the elephant is not a tail or an ear or a trunk, but is all these things and more.

Remember, nothing is IT. No one thing is IT. Everything is IT.

Commentary 22

THE FEAR OF LOVING

sychologists tell us that the fear of loving can begin with an infant, in the mother-child relationship. They speak of a tribe of Africans where the child is not allowed to lie in the mother's arms or be wrapped in a soft blanket, but is put in a rough basket and made to take its milk in an erect position. They say that because of these and other actions the child develops into a hostile, unloving person which, of course, is what the tribe wants. The pattern of these people is one of warring, possessing and taking advantage.

The moment of conception has an impact also. The sex act can be put into two categories, one of lust and one of loving. A vibrational force field is involved in everything: if a child is conceived in lust,

rather than love, a pattern of negation immediately surrounds it. As the fetus develops, the child, who might be called a biological by-product, perceives the vibration of unwanted. The parents may or may not want the child. Negative vibrations surround that bit of life and this helps to develop an unloving person.

If you deny a plant adequate nutriment, sunshine and water, you'll have a dwarfed and unhappy plant. The lack, for humans, of the essential nutriment of Love results in dwarfed or unhappy person. It's result is a fear to love, a fear of Loving. What can be done to overcome this fear or can it be over come? There is nothing that cannot be overcome. Life may be likened to a big blackboard — everything that is written upon that board can be erased or altered or reconstructed.

Someone who hasn't been loved and hasn't loved but who seeks to be more loving can begin by projecting thoughts of love to others perhaps in a very small way. It is like wading into a stream. If you think the water is cold you can put your toe in first and then your ankle. After a while, you'll find

yourself splashing in the water with your whole body. Love is very much like this. You can go about it gradually and in time you find yourself being consumed by it. You find yourself being dedicated to Love, being a part of, a channel for Love. But that first step is most important; that first decision to put your toe into the water, to begin the act.

It has been written, "That which we fear, we draw unto ourselves." Those who fear Love often draw Love about them but because of this fear it does not become a part of them. They do not know what to do with a loving environment. Fear tears apart, it twists, bends, covers up, destroys. Love unfolds, strengthens, affirms, builds. Since we are all children of God, and God is Love, then we are children of Love. Don't turn your back upon it. Receive it with open arms, in joy, aware that intrinsically you are conceived of the great energy of unconditional Love.

Commentary 23

BLIND FAITH

s Faith blind? When you speak of blindness, it implies being without sight, without vision. Yet, if anything has sight, Faith does. Its sight is not limited to today or tomorrow but is connected to infinity, eternity. It is born from True Sight, not the sight we usually refer to as vision. Ordinary sight is a way of looking in a three dimensional world. As you go into the other dimensions you find inner vision, the True Vision and from this is linked Creation. From Creation springs Manifestation. It would be a shallow world if there was not an inner way of Seeing. From it came the great paintings, the great buildings and sculpture, the great music, great literature, and that which we refer to as the creative arts.

It was written years ago, "By their faith you shall know them." Many people take this to have reference to a particular church organization. This is not so. Faith is a way of life; a way of life born out of an inner conviction which comes into its maturity when it becomes part of your actions. It could be restated, "By their actions you shall know them." Faith, in essence, is action. The person who talks about his faith but does nothing about it has little of it.

Faith and shovels move mountains. Faith is the inner conviction, the shovel represents the action. Coupled together, tremendous things occur. The faith of a few people created the United States. This is faith mobilized into action, transmuted. This is vital to the process of living. As you transmute Faith into action, you transmute Love into action, and it is part of the raising of the vibration, of entering into higher consciousness.

Faith is good for everyone. But, if you have faith in something, do something about it. If you don't have faith in anything, you're a poor man. Get some. Act upon it.

Commentary 24

A NICKEL IN YOUR POCKET

retend you are walking down the street and you have a nickel in your pocket. There's a sign in an ice cream parlor that says, ICE CREAM CONES 5 CENTS. You are very attracted to that ice cream cone. What is the spiritual lesson?

Everything has a price. You get nothing for nothing, that's a Law of the Universe. Also, there is an important sequence to this event. You made a decision. You had to pay a nickel before you got the ice cream cone. This is something that many people don't understand. They expect things out of life without first paying the price. But you must pay the price first.

It's the same with everything in life. If you want happiness, first make somebody else happy. In

giving of yourself and in giving of happiness, it returns. It was written many, many years ago, "Seek and ye shall find." You must seek — that's the price — and then you will find. This process creates a balanced situation.

All well-lived life is good business and good business is a situation wherein all parties gain. This is the essence of good dealings; you gain and they gain. If you take advantage of others, then that's not good dealing. Yet, every day much business is done on an out-of balanced basis. Too often it's "How much can I take from this person and how little can I give?"

The key is to give and not necessarily in terms of dollars. Rather, it's in terms of attitudes, in terms of thoughts, in terms of all the ramifications that go to make up You. If you prime the pump, the water will flow. This is the lesson to be learned for those who complain, "I'm not happy, nobody loves me; I don't have this, I don't have that." They haven't learned to set the things in motion. They must pay their nickel and then they will get the ice cream cone.

If you seek something from life then, first, decide what it is that you want. Is it happiness, enlightenment, truth, love? Secondly, reach into your pocket or your consciousness, or your heart, and pay the price. Thirdly, you get the reward or balancing factor. When things are in equilibrium, life is flowing nicely. When things get out of balance, then you'll have troubles, debts. What are you going to do with the nickel in your pocket?

8

Let not your quest or search
be like a garbage can that collects
everything...

Commentary 25

THE POWER OF CHOICE

eople often operate on the premise that the substance of their lives comes from somewhere. They don't know where that somewhere is, but it is outside themselves. I'm sure you've heard, "I'm stuck with this situation, this is what the Fates have decreed." This is a false premise because there is no way a life must be. Life will be as you make it, as you structure it. A life is a very malleable thing like a piece of clay or a piece of putty. You can take this and do almost anything you want to it.

There is a blueprint for each person's life but within that blueprint there are many possibilities, fluctuations, ramifications, many areas in which to operate. As an example, say that you are supposed to go from Los Angeles to New York. There is

nothing that defines how long it must take or how you should go. You can rollerskate, swim, stop and loiter beside the way, fly, drive, etc. You have the power of choice. You can regulate the type of travel and the speed. Everyone's blueprint for life is to expand consciousness, to grow, to become more aware of who and what we really are and to live in accordance with it, but the way you grow is up to the individual. Unfortunately, many people choose to grow in a rather painful manner. They make it rough for themselves and then they want to blame somebody else or insist that the Fates have dealt unfairly. A more realistic attitude is that each person has the choice to take what flowers they want from the garden. They have the choice of pricking their fingers or not; or, if they don't want the flowers, they can move on to other areas.

Life is a constant choice. It is a choice from the very beginning. We even choose our parents. When you can say, "I made the choice," you've reached a certain maturity. Then if you don't like what you have chosen, you can rechoose, restructure or change the situation.

As you expand your consciousness or awareness,

you learn to make better choices and this is an important part of development. You make the better choices when you make them intuitively, from within instead of from without. You'll find that if you make choices with the intellect, you often end up banging your head against the wall. But if you choose from the intuitive point of view, from that something deep within, you have found the choice that transcends a psychological or intellectual standpoint. There are choices on many, many levels, and it's always a growing, an expanding, a polishing that's taking place. However, you can determine how fast or how slow this growth is to take place.

The constant pattern of life and living is change. There is no way that things have to be. There is nothing that is not within your grasp, nothing that is impossible. You have but to choose and once you have done so you set wheels in motion to bring things about. No one else is dictating your life. You are dictating it yourself. You are the author. You are the captain of your ship. You can go as fast or as slow as you want. You can steer the ship in circles if you desire. It's your life. It's your world. You have the power of choice.

Commentary 26

PERFECTION

nce there was a young disciple who bowed down before his guru and stated, "Teacher, I'm a seeker." The teacher asked, "What do you seek?" "I seek perfection," replied the disciple. "Come, I will show you perfection", said his teacher.

They wandered to a hillside where stood a beautiful pine tree. "This is perfection." The student studied the tree and his eye saw that one of the branches of the tree was withered and twisted. He said, "No, Master, that's not perfect. I see imperfections." The teacher then took him to a clearing in the forest where wild flowers grew, and reached down and picked a flower and said, "Here is perfection." The student looked at the flower, but he noticed that one of the leaves was discolored. "No, Master," he said,

"that is not perfect." Then the teacher led him to a stream and asked him to look into the water. The student saw a reflection of himself. Again the teacher said, "This is perfection," and the student restated, "No, Master, that is not perfect."

The teacher sat by the side of the stream next to the pupil and said, "You came seeking perfection and you saw a tree, but it was not perfect. You saw the flower and you saw the reflection, and these, you said, were not perfect. When you seek perfection in your heart, then you will find it."

Everything is in a state of perfection, but as long as you seek perfection in the physical world, you will not find it. Somewhere, in the finest statue in the world, there is a crack. Somewhere in the finest symphony, there is a harsh note. Somewhere in the sunset, there will be a streak of black. Everything we experience from a physical point of view is unfolding toward a revelation of perfection just as we are growing, expanding, perfecting. If you seek that which is pristine, pure, whole, then do not seek it in the physical world since everything here is evolving toward that state.

You will recall the story of the young man who disagreed violently with his father. He thought him stupid, and yet after the lad had matured he found his father to be very wise. The eyes that you now use for looking will one day become eyes of seeing not the surface, but that which is beyond the surface. And, if you see deeply enough, you will find the perfection in all things, in the Essence, in the Reality. Do not become concerned with surface; it is merely a shadow of perfection, an imperfect reflection. Go within and there you will find the harmony you are seeking.

Commentary 27

ENTERING THE SILENCE

s you enter into a time of quiet, think of it as a most significant time. Much of your day is given to going here, there, chatting, talking, all the thousands of things that you do. This is important because you live in a physical world with physical properties, physical bodies and physical needs. Yet, there is another part of you, call it what you will, the inner you. The outward manifestation is like the icing on a cake. There can be thick ones, thin ones, of decorations, swirls and yet, this is not the cake. The icing which is "you" is not You. True, it is the overt you, the physical you, but to balance it you must be aware of the non-physical You, the You that knows no pettiness, no limitations, no boundaries. The You of the Silence.

Most of your energy patterns are expended in the manifested world, but in the quiet times you reach

out to the Cosmos and feed from this invisible realm. It is not a substance that can be weighed or measured and yet it is very real. As you feed the inner self, your totality comes into balance. This is important.

You can be unbalanced in either direction. You can be concerned with the outer world and shrink the within until it is insignificant. Or, you can refuse to admit there is a world about you and become a recluse and spend your time in contemplation. Both of these extremes form an imbalance. You need time to enter the Silence, to feed, to strengthen, to expand your inner resources, just as you need time to be involved with the outer world. As you blend these two into a pattern of doing you become whole. It's then that life takes on a new perspective.

For a few moments close your eyes. Relax. Lay aside the cares and the woes and frustrations that you might have claimed. They don't belong to you. Breathe deeply and remember as you breathe that you're breathing the breath of God. Not of some mysterious or anthropomorphic entity who sits on a throne but, rather, of the God within, the God

surrounding. There's nothing that you can conceive of that is not God. You have your being within the Divine Mind.

As you enter the Silence and become aware of this magnificence, know that you are being recharged, rejuvenated, spiritually uplifted. Know who you really are. You're not a name, you're not a body, you are the Universe itself. Every marvel in the world is within you. Go within and touch the wonder, the beauty, the joy. Let your life spread this about like a farmer planting seeds. Then watch the flowers and the harvest that comes forth.

In the Silence, tomorrow does not exist — only now — this Golden Moment.

Commentary 28

CHILDREN OF THE RAINBOW

[T]here is a legend in a Polynesian culture [th]at their people are the Children of [th]e Rainbow. How true this statement [is]. It applies to you as well. In essence, [a]uras are little rainbows. Not the same [as] the ones in the sky, but they are

[I]n a rainbow there are seven areas, seven segments of color: red, orange, yellow, green, blue, indigo, and violet. Each of you are composed of those seven segments, as well. The seven chakras.

Your birth was within the red spectrum. In the aura it is seen as the color of generation, the red molten lava. One drop of red molten lava became you. The orange represents your energy. The yellow, your

intellect. Green is the balance. Blue is the spirituality towards which we all should strive.

Indigo is the intuitive color. Violet is the high spiritual. Both the red and the violet are consuming fires. The Bible speaks often of Light or of letting your Light shine forth. Think of it as letting your rainbow shine out.

As you go out into the world today, remember to let your Light shine. You are a Child of the Rainbow.

9

Everything is in degrees...
if a person steps off a ten-inch step, he is not harmed, but if he steps off a step that is a thousand times ten-inches, he is killed...

Commentary 29

WHAT DO YOU WANT FOR CHRISTMAS

When you are first asked what you want for Christmas, does it start a flow of colorful patterns streaming through your consciousness? A word may trigger a barrage of images and ideas leading to all sorts of results. "What do you really want for Christmas?"

One of the nicest things would be to have peace within yourself and peace around you. Also, it would be nice to have Love. Service to mankind would be most self-fulfilling.

Interestingly enough, these are not things that anybody else can give you. They are things you must give yourself. If there is to be peace, this peace has to start within you. If you are to have love, you should be more loving. If you are to be of service to mankind, only you can do it. And, what will you serve.

Often an innocent statement (service to mankind) is made without much thought to what it means. What really do you have to offer, to serve? You wouldn't offer a guest an empty cup. So, if you wish to serve mankind, and you are members of mankind, you should start with yourself. You should fortify yourself spiritually. It is then that you will have something to serve, something to give.

These things I am speaking of don't come tied up in red and green packages. Though material gifts are good also, they have their place as tokens and symbols. With all this in mind, what do you want for Christmas? What can you do? What can you give? Be still, go within, find your answer.

Commentary 30

THE NATURE OF REALITY

hen we speak of Reality, we are speaking in terms of the eternal, of something that does not have limitations, that knows no boundaries of time and space. A sense of reverence is involved. In reading some of the New Age literature, it's apparent the word "reality" refers to a more shallow reality and it is important to distinguish between these two conceptions. One might be called a little 'r', and the other a big 'R'. The little r's are concerned with the realities of the moment, problems, personal visions and feelings. The other, a capital R, is reflected in terms of Love, God, the Essence of all things.

When you think of reality as pertaining to the third dimension, it's a little 'r'. It is of the moment and is

limited. Momentary things slip by as the clock ticks. But, when you ponder upon words like Love and God, which are two expressions for the same thing, this prompts feelings and patterns of foreverness. An Essence knows no boundaries, an Essence flows. It is of Reality.

As you focus on Reality, 'R', you'll find yourself spreading your horizons, you'll find yourself in an unlimited state. As you go about your day, be concerned with the little realities that come and go, but keep paramount in your thoughts the big Reality. It has no beginning and no end. It is timeless as, in essence, you are timeless. The small 'r' is only a minute part of the big 'R'. Use the former (r) to transcend to the latter (R).

Commentary 31

LETTING GO

editation is a time of release, of letting go, a time of detachment. Usually you cling tightly to problems, to fears and frustrations, and wear them like a garment. You get used to them and don't want to take them off. Yet there comes a time when it becomes necessary to unload, to become at-one with the Magnificence that lies within each human being, to see oneself not as a dwarf but as a giant; not as someone who is imprisoned, but as someone who is free. When you enter into meditation and let go, a rebirthing takes place, a restructuring, a fortifying. You'll find that if you let go for only a few moments, the weight that seemed to be very heavy shrinks in size because you are no longer feeding it energy.

Today, as you enter the world within, cut yourself loose from everything that is weighing upon you. Visualize yourself taking off a suit of armor that is very heavy and throwing it aside. It's no longer necessary to do battle. Breathe freely. As you enter into the Silence and direct your attention inward rather than outward, you'll find that there is a vast place of calm, perfection and balance.

It's easy to be concerned with something on the other side of the mountain, a place where the grass grows greener. Yet you can meditate, go within and reach the greenest place of all, the tabernacle within. Here, you'll find the answers, the strength. It is all there. You need only BE STILL AND KNOW. Find God, the God within. There is nothing to seek that you do not already have. There is no question that does not have its answer within you. Release. Let go.

Commentary 32

PINE NUTS

Once there was a guru who tied up his goat every evening as he was about to talk to his disciples because the animal would get in the way. The man died, years went by, and even though the people had forgotten his teachings, every evening they tied up a goat. Before chapel service I relax and take a bubble bath. I look forward to the bubble bath for it is a special time of receptivity for me. Maybe a hundred years from now people will take a bubble bath expecting something special to happen.

Anyway, as I was lying back in my bubble bath in a meditative state, I was reflecting on Leon, my teacher, and the moments we had had together. These were very meaningful times, very happy times, very satisfying times to me. I came to him frequently with things that were perplexing.

On a particular day, I told him about pine nuts and how, as a child, I liked to gather the seeds from certain pine trees. In Arizona the trees grow in the north and you can pick them only at certain times. Transportation was not as it is today and it was a long arduous journey to where the trees were. I would go into the forest for hours and hours to gather them. At the end of the day, with much work, I would have gathered only a few. One day I asked my teacher, Leon, if it was worth all the effort. His face lit up, he got twinkly Santa Claus-eyes and his words had a sparkle to them. But, before I tell you his answer, I'm going to tell you another story.

There are people at the Foundation that print our monthly newsletter. This takes many, many hours and sometimes there are problems, the press may get over-inked, etc. The staff works hard and they say to themselves, "Is it worth it?" Then a few days go by and we receive a letter from someone that says, "What a great newsletter. I was at my end when the newsletter came. It gave me a new lift. Thank you." That's the pine nuts, isn't it? Sometimes the reward may seem rather small in proportion to other things.

When I asked Leon if the pine nuts gathering was

worth it, he gave me a very profound answer. Think about it. He said, "Well, I guess it all depends on how much you like pine nuts."

10

Be not concerned with what you are getting out of life, but what you are giving it...
It is truly a privilege to give...

Commentary 33

YOU

eople talk a lot about the four-letter words, but I would like to focus attention on an important word that has only three letters. It's the word Y-O-U, YOU. In the endeavor called living, or life, we get concerned with that which is "out there," and sometimes we don't give enough consideration to the Self. While I am not encouraging anyone to be narcissistic, I'm not encouraging anyone to put themselves aside either.

You know the story of the man who searched the wide world over looking for God. He went to Tibet and India, the Vatican, and all the holy places. He went high, he went low, but he couldn't find Him anywhere. One morning when he was shaving, he looked into the mirror and there was God looking at him through his own eyes. This is a very

meaningful story, for individuality is very meaningful. You are very meaningful.

How often do you remind yourself that you are unique? Regardless of what a mess you make out of life or how unsuccessful you are at it, no one is going to do it quite like you. No one else has your fingerprints, feet, brain, etc. You are a unique creation. You may find someone who resembles you, has eyes or a smile a bit like yours, but you won't find a duplication.

YOU has three letters and is structurally significant. It is the Trinity movement. It's a powerful unit, a building unit.

The first letter, Y, is the yoke. It joins, ties together. Your immediate image may be the wooden piece used to join animals together. What you get yoked up with, or unify with, is very significant because that with which you identify, of course, affects you.

The second letter is O. This is the symbol of God, Perfection, Cosmos, Creation. It is the circular movement, round without beginning and without end, continuous.

Thirdly, the letter U. The cup. The chalice has many significances but, basically, it represents a challenge, it holds. This challenge may be filled or emptied.

As you combine these structural significances of the word itself, you'll see that YOU is unique and important. You are important, you are unique. You are filled with a precious substance. If you have a jar and fill it with whatever is most precious, you will take care of it. And yet, YOU, you yourself, are filled with the divine substance called God and there is a deep responsibility that goes along with this. Each person (and each of us is a YOU) comes to this existence to make a unique contribution.

Give more thought to yourself, to what you do, to what you think, to what you believe, to who you are, to the yoke, the circle, the cup. Where YOU are, God is there also.

Commentary 34

LAW OF BALANCE

It's common that either you or someone close to you owes someone, something. It seems we are always beholden to someone. And, after all, if we didn't ask to be born and if we have to be here, why couldn't we be born to a family of means and not have any obligations to anyone else?

Birth is not just due to an ejaculation when a sperm happens to find its way down a narrow canal to unite with an egg. It is a long involved process, but YOU start it. You ask to be born. The reasons may be many, but, actually, you request it. As to what life owes you, you may expect back exactly what you put out. If you give to life, life will give to you. As with a bank account, you have the right and privilege to take what you put in. Nothing in equals

nothing out, a zero. So, you are where you are because you requested it. It is necessary for your growth. And, what you are getting out of it is exactly what you are putting into it.

This is a law, the Law of Balance. You'll find it present in everything on every level. It is the Yin/Yang. It's a balancing, a compensating, a basic law.

In the ancient Sanskrit writings there's a saying, "The man who sings songs shall have songs sung unto him." Christianity adopted this and from it came the famous, "Cast your bread upon the waters..." This is like priming the pump. Many of you don't come from the pump-priming days, but the way to begin the flow of water was to first pour some in the pump. This is what we have to do in life, we have to prime the pump.

This is applicable in all facets of living, in your doing, your feeling, in all your transactions. It is a very difficult law to reckon with because, being like children, we want to take short cuts or cheat. We want to get away with something and if it doesn't work to our benefit, we complain. If only this principle could be remembered in all dealings.

As people grow older, they begin having aches and pains. This is a result of what was put into the body. It is a result of diet and thought. It is a balancing of what went before.

Everything can be equated to this principle. It's difficult because it's easier to look to others to justify our inadequacies. You've heard, "They did this to me, they did that to me." The truth is that no one can do anything to you. You can only do it to yourself. The responsibility is on your shoulders for the life you have although this is not always easy to accept.

You can't always trace how it all comes about. It may be very complex and involved. The intangibles of life can't always be traced to a tangible incident, it may take another form than just tit for tat. If you give $10 to charity one week, you may not receive $10 from somewhere the next week. You will get your $10 worth but it might come in a different way. It might take a year, it might take three years or more. You cannot really predict how it will come back, but it does come back.

Have you ever wondered how people get away with things? Actually, no one gets away with

anything. It's all recorded in each individual's cosmic account. You might think you can pull the shades and no one can see you, that you are having a thought no one can peek in to, yet it's all being recorded and it balances itself.

This is what Karma is about. It is a balancing situation and it can't always be taken care of in one life pattern. Sometimes it takes many life patterns for the process to be completed, but there will be a balancing. That's the law. That's the principle. It is not a law of my creation or your creation, but it is the law of Creation itself. You can't escape it. It's nothing to fear. The solution to this equalizing process is to see how much of a positive force you put out, to see how much you can prime the pump, to see how much you can give.

Some people's lives are plus, some are a minus, and some are a zero. This is the difference between living and existing. Many people exist, few people live. Existing is just a getting by, a zero, or if that person is a real taker, a minus. To just exist is a rather painful sort of thing, slow with a monotonous vibration to it. Living takes on a different beat, a different rhythm. Living comes from within and is

giving and joyous. It can be equated to a beautiful fountain, bubbling, sparkling, a reaching out. Existence relates to a pond that is cluttered with all sorts of debris. Both the pond and the fountain are water, yet one is reaching up and moving while the other is stagnating. Neither is good and neither is bad, you can't equate them on those terms. They just are. But each person has the choice of being a stagnating pond or being a fountain. To live is to be a plus.

This is what Jesus was saying: "Let your light shine out..." When you're living and giving of yourself, there is a light that shines from you. How many people have you seen who are radiant, glowing? The ones who have this nice countenance are giving-people, serving-people. It's not all a dollar and cents thing, for that's one of the least important ways to give. It's easy to write a check and say, "Well, I've done my bit." But to commit your life to something or to give of your time and strength and labors, that's different.

Today, ponder this principle of Balance or Cosmic Equation. Do some introspection yourself and ask,

"Am I priming the pump?" If you're not or if you're just barely doing so, what more can you do to prime it? What more can you do to give? What more can you do to love? What more can you do to Be, to express what you really Are.

Remember, you are dealing with a law, a principle. The idea is to work with a principle, not against it. To work with it, to mesh, to meld, to allow yourself to be. One of your reasons for being on the earth plane is to gain balance. When you have reached the point of balance, you have reached Perfection, a Crystallization of Essence – YOU ARE. This is the process you are involved in: a being and becoming, a coming into Being.

Commentary 35

LOVE

On February 14th of each year we have a holiday called Saint Valentine's Day. On this day we pay homage to Love. Because it is difficult to relate to things we cannot see, we give Love a shape, and then since every shape must have a color, we color it. A red heart becomes our symbol of Love.

But on February 15th, we put away the symbol for another year. But is Love a piece of red paper that can be folded and put away? I'm sure you have heard someone say, "I don't love him/her anymore." Is Love something that you can turn on and turn off?

Love is a flow, it is a verb, it is an action, a way of life. It is not a day or an hour. It is not something to be put in your pocket, to be taken out at will. Love

knows no time, no distance, no dimension. Love always WAS and always WILL BE. It is. Every man, every woman, whether they realize it or not, comes into this life expression to give, for life is a dedication. When you give of yourself, you are giving Love. It has ten thousand faces and it permeates the universe.

Some men think that if they display love they will be looked upon as weak. Rather, Love is a strength. Some people think that to display love makes them look foolish or that if they give Love that it will not be returned. But the problem here is whether the love is the tangible type of love with possession attached to it or Love of a higher nature that exudes from an individual and represents a cosmic energy of the highest order. The former is temporary, shallow, subject to the whims of the third dimension. The latter is eternal, with depth, and can be felt as real and with strength. One needs to be fed and is taking, the other feeds itself and is giving. Think of the caption under a picture from Father Flanagan's Boys Town showing a young lad with a crippled boy on his shoulders: "He's not heavy, Father, he's my brother." Is this a foolish and taking love or a real and giving Love? Is the strong boy looking for something in return?

There was a song popular years ago that said "Love makes the world go 'round." This is a universal principle. Without Love there would be disintegration. Love is a cohesive force, it holds things together. It builds, it strengthens, it purifies and unifies. Love can open any door and solve any problem. It gives.

My valentine to you reads: Love is always and always is forever. It's for every day of the year.

Commentary 36

WORDS

arly in your studies towards a higher life, you will be confronted with the question, "What is right and what is wrong?" Actually, they're just words that are very much misused by the human race. It's our attempt to weigh and measure.

If you had a gun and killed someone, society would declare that you had done a wrong. However, if you were in a uniform and in battle, you would have done a right. Is one of these actions wrong and the other right?

Cosmically speaking, there is no right or wrong. Things are. Words are third dimensional tools, man's invention. Because something is proclaimed to be wrong or right doesn't mean it is so. It's only man's interpretation, not that of the universe. It is, however, a good indication of man's approach to life and his level of consciousness.

When you go beyond words, you enter into the Realm of Truth, Light, Wisdom. True Wisdom has never been written. Words are for the third dimension. Wisdom is of a higher nature or vibration. The moment you write or speak "Truth," you reduce its vibration to that of the intellect and it becomes limited.

The more you talk about "Truth," the further you get from it. You must seek that which is beyond words. True, you have to be practical and you must speak when people have spoken to you. We find it necessary to communicate with words, but we must take them for what they are and know that beyond them lies that which is Real. Someday, words will no longer be necessary.

If you go into the derivation of the words 'right' and 'wrong', take them back to their original representations, the meanings today are very different than they once were. Original meanings of words change, languages change, but Reality doesn't. Reality always was, always IS. This is why it is necessary to meditate, to go beyond words into the world of Silence, into the Reality where things do not have labels, do not have limitations, where they are pristine.

Mankind is a contaminator. There is pollution of mind and body, the environment, the world with words. Many of the social, religious, and philosophical structures are based upon arbitrary labels of right and wrong. Examine your own thoughts and notice how many times in the day you apply the concepts of right and wrong. In your daily activities, as you hear and use words, accept them for what they are. Don't let them be the guideposts for your spiritual exploration because if you do, you'll find dead-ends. Rather, go within, into the wordless world to find your direction. There will be no dead-ends, only a straight path that goes up and up and up. Cosmically speaking, words are valueless.

11

Work with the laws
of the universe and you will
have everything...
Work against them and you
will have nothing,
because you will cut off
the flow...

Commentary 37

GOD IS THERE ALSO

t the Foundation we end each meditation and gathering with these words: "We are surrounded in Light, we are surrounded in Love, we are enfolded in the Peace Profound, and where we are, God is there also." The last part of that statement is especially important.

All over the world you find people in conflict with each other. Some are building things, while others are tearing things down. Some are in search of God by taking downers or uppers. Others are in monastic settings, some meditate, go to church, and study. Human beings go through all sorts of gyrations in search of God.

We really don't have to search for God. We just have to come to the realization that God is within.

We take God with us everywhere we go. If we can accept that belief, then shouldn't we start acting in accordance with it? If we have within us the most wonderful of wonderfuls, the most beautiful of beautifuls, the highest of the highs, then how can we chase after, or use bizarre means to find, God?

Most people do not love themselves. Not standing in front of a mirror throwing kisses at the reflection; rather, loving what you really are, realizing that you are a manifestation of God. Everyone is a part of God and so long as you remove yourself from that fact, you will search and never find. Stop searching and start being who you really are. Remember, "Where you are, God is there also."

Commentary 38

MOTHERHOOD

oday we gather together to ponder upon, and pay tribute to, the concept and reality of Motherhood and its significance in the Grand Design. Here is, from a structured point of view or essence, what Motherhood reflects.

In the Tarot there is a card illustrating a mother pelican with many baby pelicans. They sit on a nest on top of pilings. The young pelicans are without food and the mother pulls meat from her chest to feed her young. This is the meaning of Motherhood: Sacrifice.

History reflects that much has been sacrificed in the name of Motherhood. Think of the thousands of women who have given their lives to give birth to

their young. A father never dies in childbirth, it's the mother who makes the sacrifice. Think of the many mothers who have, in the depression times, laid aside their meal to feed their youngsters. How many mothers placed pieces of cardboard in their shoes so their children could have new ones. There's sacrifice even in the prenatal state. The fetus pulls nutriment from the body of the woman. It's said a woman is never as beautiful as when she first walks down the aisle as a bride. But when she first looks upon her new born child there is a look on her face, a glow, her eyes beaming forth, all with meaning and purpose. It's a link in a flowing chain and, without that link, the chain of mankind would be broken. It is a part that we all play at some time, for as you know, incarnation patterns allow us to take many roles.

There is much talk now about women's liberation. Some of the individuals shouting the loudest never have been and never will be mothers in this lifetime. They really don't appreciate motherhood or the sacrifice that goes with it. And yet, a liberation of motherhood is important in the cosmic sense, for as one enters the state of motherhood, a type of liberation goes with it. Not a militant type that is

cheap and coarse, but rather a self-fulfilling type that is emancipated and beautiful.

As you meditate, do so in appreciation of a role each of us will at some time play, this role called Motherhood. As you celebrate this day, pay tribute to the mothers of the world and pay tribute to yourself as well.

Commentary 39

SIMILARITIES

he important things in life are often the so-called unimportant and may go unnoticed. Things that appear to be radically different may, in essence, be very similar.

Human beings appear to be very different, but it is good to examine their similarities in many ways and on many levels. We're all pretty much the same: two legs, two arms, two ears, etc. We come in various shapes and sizes and this makes it interesting. If you go into the structure of man, you'll find that man is what can be called a five-organism. A human being is a star with five points (two arms, two legs, head). Stars come into the world to give light. "Let your light shine out before you," said Jesus. Everyone has a light to project but we get caught up in things that interfere with it, in the

insignificant differences that really don't matter. Wars are fought over differences, peace is accompanied by similarities.

We're coming into a time of great testing. The weak will perish and the strong will survive. There is only one real strength, the spiritual strength within us. And as we look at the similarities in people, we start building this strength and love. It is like a chain. At first there are separate links, but when we put them together and we give them a bond, they have a unity, they have a strength. In the days ahead, strength is going to be very important, because there are going to be obstacles, barriers, confusions, upheavals to overcome. The strong will survive.

Hands are made to hold. Bodies are made to hug. People came into existence to work together, to meet challenges together, to learn from one another. They came to grow, not to enervate themselves by examining the tiny, insignificant differences, but by working together. There is only one Spirit, the Spirit flowing within all of us.

The major religions are thought to be of separate philosophies, but, in essence, they are all the same.

"All things whatsoever ye would that men should do to you, do ye even so to them," said Jesus. Confucius says, "Do not unto others what you would not they should do unto you." Buddha speaks, "In five ways should a clansman minister to his friends and familiars - by generosity, courtesy and benevolence, by treating them as he treats himself, and by being as good as his word." Mohammed tells us, "No one of you is a believer until he loves for his brother what he loves for himself."

There are common threads in all major philosophies. A thread may seem insignificant, but threads make ropes, links make chains, and people holding hands working together make Beauty and Love.

Commentary 40

GRAINS OF SAND

he world is going through many chaotic patterns. People are shouting and fighting, burning flags and throwing rocks. Such activities are a sign of ignorance. Not ignorance in terms of two and two makes four, but ignorance in terms of the folly of such actions. Someday, it will be learned that only constructive actions really matter, only the things done in love. Everything else takes up space and adds to the clutter of the cosmos.

There are many people who look to the lofty mountains and make plans to climb. Wouldn't it be nice if they would first take care of the grains of sand in their shoes? Isn't it better to first take care of your own home before you attempt to take care of someone else's?

First things first. You need to be very concerned with the moment and to handle each in the most positive, most loving, and most creative way you can. Take care of the grains of sand, and then, when the time comes, you'll cross the mountains.

Commentary 41

A SOLID FOUNDATION

What should you strive towards? You should not strive for anything. This is not to say you should give up and resign yourself to the 'fate of life', but that striving is not the key. Ask people what they want out of life and laughingly, somewhat embarrassed, most often they'll say, "Money, and the comforts first, and then I'll do something of a more lasting nature." Isn't this backwards? If you were to ask a carpenter how to start a house, wouldn't he reply that you need a good, solid foundation before you build the rest of the structure? First things first.

Could it be that what was written thousands of years ago still holds true today? The advice given was, "Seek ye first the Kingdom of Heaven and all things shall be added unto you." What is the Kingdom of

Heaven? The Kingdom of Heaven lies within. It has to do with flowing rather than striving. This is not just a semantic difference. It's a vibrational difference.

For example, a fox trot and a waltz are not the same. They have different motions, different vibrations, different rhythms. Flowing and striving are two different things. Striving is very angular, sharp, bulldozing, getting ahead no matter what the cost. Flowing is working with the rhythms of nature, cooperating, blending, being aware of the harmony of all things.

The answers don't lie in temporary items such as a new car, new house or new wife. The answer isn't in an injection of some chemical or puffing on some plant. The answer lies within you. "Seek ye first the Kingdom of Heaven and all things shall be added unto you." This is the basis for a Solid Foundation.

12

You do not seek happiness, you become happiness and it becomes you...

Commentary 42

WHO'S GOT THE TRUTH

Everyone is looking for something, hoping somebody can give them the answer to what they ask or chase after. People seek gurus expecting that, through perseverance, they'll be given the Truth. Actually, nobody can give you anything of a spiritual nature. You can be given a loaf of bread, a pat on the back, a lovely smile, or any number of third dimensional items. But from a cosmic point of view, nobody can give you anything of a higher nature. You already have it and the secret is to find it and realize that you have it.

Nobody can give you an answer you already have. It's all there within you. Someone may help you find a key to trigger the awareness within or provide you with an experience that helps to open a door to Truths. That, they can give you. Direction, yes, but answers, no.

The best method for realizing your own answers is to sit still and listen; to become in touch with the Essence that comprises us all. The answers to a greater and more fulfilling spiritual life are there, within, as you contact this energy. We've been so conditioned to the things we weigh and measure that it's difficult to shift the attention from outward manifestations to inward manifestation. This energy doesn't require a label, it's not of this dimension, but it's always there in the Silence, unlabeled.

When you're quiet, and still, you can draw upon this energy and weave it into your life. Your awareness will grow, your life will expand, you will become stronger. The Truth you already have will be known.

Commentary 43

SEEING THE MOUNTAIN

By habit we compartmentalize, label, put things into pigeon holes, little boxes. Maybe that's the only way most of us can handle life but, in doing this, something is lost. Labels limit and distort the true meaning. A prairie with trees and plants in the foreground, mountains in the distance, and sunsets for a backdrop offer a lovely picture. But when it's segmented or labeled or cut up into little pieces the one-time vast prairie becomes lost.

We do this with ideas, thoughts, almost everything with which we come in contact. If, instead of dissecting things into little patterns we could learn to think more in terms of the wholes, as the whole picture or the whole scheme, and recognize this as being perfection, although we might not be able to fully experience this perfection and this wholeness, we would have a greater understanding.

Perhaps a story my teacher, Leon, told me best conveys this: "Once upon a time there was a magnificent mountain. It was beaufiful, very high and very lofty. There was a man who lived at the base of the mountain and another man who lived a great distance from it. The man who lived close to the mountain spent his lifetime looking at all the rocks and sorting them into piles; he had the white rocks in one pile and the black rocks in another, the round rocks separate from the square ones. There were many careful piles of rocks requiring a great deal of zealous thought and labor. Each had its own use. But the man who lived far from the mountain saw it the best. Only he realized its magnificence."

It's common to become concerned with the rocks and with sorting them out, fussing and fuming, working, separating things into piles. But the mountain goes unnoticed even though it's right before your eyes. Yet it's there if you will but look. No one can do it for you, it's for your eyes to see.

Commentary 44

SYNCHRONIZATION

ome people become involved in a project in a manner they think best illustrates a positive approach, and yet, within themselves, there may be a negative thought pattern present. What happens? The project doesn't result in a positive outcome.

If two people in a boat paddle in different directions, the boat goes around in a circle. This is what most people are doing. Going in a circle. There is a clash of vibratory patterns; one pattern is pointed in one direction and the other is pointed in another direction. You might say one pattern is pointed to "no" and the other to "yes." This is a common division within the self. "I'm going to do this but I know it won't be successful", and it won't be. People don't realize that there is just as much power in the thought that they are going to do something

as there is in the action of doing it. There is the same voltage or number of units of power in one as in the other. One is in the manifested realm and one is in the unmanifested. Consequently, if you have the muscles in the body (the manifested) going one direction, and the mind silently saying it can't or shouldn't be done, you are creating a schism; two opposing pulls that present a stalemate. Sometimes people are so divided that very little happens in their lives. They complain, but they have only themselves to blame.

Consider the Olympic runners. When they are running the race everything about them is synchronized; their bodies, their minds. Everything is focused upon reaching the goal. If you could create the same interlocking efforts in your life how many goal lines could you pass, how many races could you win? In the successful man or woman, you'll find a synchronizing of energies and dedication. There is an understanding among ballet dancers that if you want to be the top ballerina you must become married to the art, totally committed.

If you are to accomplish meaningful things in life you must become synchronized, not schizophrenic and divided. "A house divided against itself will

fall." A person divided within will fall also. If you are to climb the ladder, you must climb as a total entity. The passage in the Bible that speaks of God as a jealous God is not speaking of jealousy in the ordinary sense that we know it, it is speaking of the chaos that is produced when the force of devotion is divided against itself.

Observe yourself as you transcend life. Notice how many times you're saying one thing and doing another. If you are involved in a three-ring circus you will accomplish very little.

Give this some thought in the days ahead. It's very exciting to observe yourself. You can do it. You can look at yourself and see exactly what makes you tick. When you observe thoughts going in one direction and the body in another direction, stop. The result will be chaos.

Do you remember the predictable lines in old movies many years ago? At a crucial point people would gather in a secluded place and the leader would say, "All right men, let's synchronize our watches!" This was an expected scene. The premise was, that once you organize and synchronize, you can accomplish. This same concept should be applied to your life for a positive result.

Commentary 45

BLESSING

any people take Blessing on a superficial level. They think it is just a word or a meaningless act. But a blessing has trememdous significance.

We live in a world of energy patterns many of which are of our own design. As we move through these patterns and involve ourselves with them we can be affected in either an adverse or a positive way. If our surrounding energy patterns are positive, then we are affected in this way.

There are many Biblical references to the word Blessing. Basically, here's what happens: when you send forth a blessing from the heart, from the feeling level, you send forth an energy pattern that affects the person or circumstance or object that you project it toward. There is a vibratory lifting. It also affects the person who sends it.

In many homes a blessing is a routine tradition. People eye their food and hurriedly say some words that have become monotonous and have lost their meaning. This type of blessing has little results whereas a blessing issued properly can have wondrous benefits.

Every thought and deed goes forth and comes back. Your entire life is one of projection and return. Some call this karma, it has many names. It is a boomerang effect. As you bless, you are blessed. As you go about your life and touch and come in contact with people and with everyday things, give forth a blessing from your heart. Your step will be lighter and your way will be straighter.

There is no one way to give a blessing. It should come from the heart. "Store bought" prayers or "store bought" blessings have little meanings. What you are doing when you bless is to realize within yourself the Oneness of all things, the God within all, that all things are a part of and have their being in God.

Blessing is giving realization or recognition to this principle. As you do so, there are subtle changes

that take place. The vibratory force-field that builds up affects those who come in contact with it. People walk into the house that has been blessed and say, "My, it feels good in here, this chair's comfortable, doesn't this food taste good!"

If there is a condition around you that is in disharmony, the act or pronouncement of a blessing can bring about a change. It is not a meddling thing. A blessing is not an attempt to twist or pervert or alter, rather it is a sending forth of energy that can harmonize.

Blessing is such a very simple but powerful act that it's often overlooked. Don't spend so much time "counting your blessings", give forth with them. Your every action and every encounter can become a positive one. The blessing you give will pass on and on and on. It is part of the raising of the consciousness. As you lift, so shall you be lifted.

Commentary 46

THE NEW YEAR

oday we face what is commonly called the New Year. As you may know, throughout history the calendar has been changed from its natural order. If we were to celebrate this new period accurately, we would do it at the time of the Winter Solstice.

We give tremendous import to the New Year time and assign our own significance to it. For some, it is an excuse to become intoxicated. For others, it is a time of making a so called New Year's resolution. A resolution is something that you carry forth, something that you complete, and, in essence, each day in the year should be a time of resolution. Unfortunately, these resolutions usually fade rather quickly.

From a cosmic point of view, this holiday has little or no significance. It is an invention of man for a third dimensional diversion. It's more difficult to be concerned with matters of a higher dimension and as man invents playthings, he diverts himself from the requisites of Reality.

The sun rises and sets without the help of clocks. The days come and go without the help of labels. But we like to segment and label nevertheless. This gives import within our own context. It gives us something to grasp and hold. We create tangibles for comfort.

Let the mind travel beyond the man-made limits of tangibles. Let the mind soar from the manifested into the unmanifested and absorb all that it can while it is there. Just as the roots of a plant can be bound by the confines of the container in which it is trying to grow, so also can the roots of human beings be bound by the containers in which they have placed themselves. With the New Year, it is time to free yourself from the confines in which you're growing and to plant yourself anew in the unlimited soil of the Cosmos. The consciousness will become enriched, flowing, at-one with the

Universe, at-one with the All. Rather than limit your New Year to the traditional resolutions, extend your horizon by traveling to greater heights and vistas. This New Year can be a great awakening for you.

Commentary 47

PROPER PERSPECTIVE

The world today has a chaotic vibration. As you read various periodicals and listen to the media, there is much talk of conflicts and shortages. There is great turbulence and the corresponding chaotic vibrations. The chaos will increase. Those who are prepared for this time period will survive. Those who are not prepared may perish. Each individual must prepare himself for this challenging period, not by remaining status quo with the same inflexible patterns, but by growing, changing, and developing a character to adequately cope with that which is ahead.

What can you do to transcend this chaos? Go within, there you will find stability, peace, direction and pristine silence. Within each of you there is a place of stability untouched by outward

manifestation. Even though the turbulence may build and seem unbearable at times, remember that no matter how stormy the ocean may appear, it is calm just below the surface. The appearance on the surface need not consume you. You can find stability and peace within.

Today, reflect upon your inner peace. Put appearances in their proper perspective. You have it all. It's a matter of coming in contact with it.

Commentary 48

ONENESS

A few weeks ago I spent a morning in the gift shop. Ordinarily that is not my function, but on that particular day everyone else was busy. I didn't mind, I enjoy being there. It is a nice place with a lot of color, a happy little place. Before long a young man entered the shop. I took one look at his aura and said, "Oh, Oh!" On the outside he had the 'clean' look. He was well scrubbed; his skin gleamed. But his aura showed him to be narrow-minded, confused and frightened. Under one arm, he grasped a large black book. He introduced himself and asked me if the Foundation teachings were based on the Bible. I said, "Yes, and no, depending on how you look at it." We talked further.

The people who are very Bible-oriented have many scripture references. This is all right, but it's

confusing to give exact literal interpretation to something that has been rewritten and rewritten, translated, edited. It's the essence that is important, the message, not the words.

The young man referred to the Bible as the "Word of God," and I queried, "Was it not written by man or men?" "Yes, it was, but it was dictated by God." Although I knew it was going to make him angry, I asked, "Aren't the New York Times and Playboy magazine written by men and dictated by God, also?" He got a very flushed look on his face. He was furious. "Oh, no!", he said, "Those are dictated by Satan!."

We talked further but there was very little rapport in our exchange. It was apparent, however, that his duality GOD vs. SATAN is the very thing that is contrary to the book that he carries with him. It contains many references to "Let thine eye be single," or "The Oneness," "The One Path." Similar references can be found in the teachings of all the Illumined Ones that have been upon the earth: Buddha, Confucius, Mohammed, Zoroaster, etc. This schism in the young man is not limited to him alone. It can be found in many places. It can be

found within you and it must be resolved before you can grow and transcend to greater Spiritual Truth.

Collective mankind has a schizophrenic viewpoint. There are neat piles for the clean wash and neat piles for the dirty wash. There are the good guys with the white hats and the bad guys with the black hats. But you must reach the point where you can say black and white are two parts of a whole, two aspects, two ramifications, two viewpoints. But, they still represent the whole. Within the circle, there is the Yin and the Yang. Both are needed or there would not be a circle.

You have to reach the point where you realize that all questions and all answers are part of the same thing. All things, all concepts come forth from the One Source. Because you can't understand something or because it is not of your liking, should it be labeled bad, should you try to destroy it? When you destroy something outside yourself, you destroy something within yourself. If your brother falls, a part of you falls also. Mankind — individual units, yes — different sizes, colors, all sorts of specifications, but all part of One.

Yet how many times in our daily lives do we divide? "The good things about us and the bad, the right things in the world and the wrong." It has been written, "A house divided against itself will fall." This is a true statement. Once you take something and divide it, it loses its energy, its power, its unity, its force field is divided. Go back to the old custom of breaking bread when someone comes to your home. It was not written that you divide the bread, that you cut the bread, but that you break the bread. This act is a performance of sharing, not a dividing as such.

In the days ahead, give careful attention to your divisive thought patterns. Seek a reformation of ideas and concepts that express Oneness and not division. As this occurs, you will notice tremendous growth taking place. You will begin to understand that all you see, feel, touch, comprehend, and all that you cannot comprehend, is God and that you have your being within the Divine Mind. You will feel the power of the Universe surge through you and know that there really is no division. You are whole. All is one.

Commentary 49

KING SOLOMON

ing Solomon lived a long time ago and became well known as a wise man. The following comes from Judaic mythology and reflects upon a time when King Solomon was visiting the court of a very influential queen.

Once upon a time, a very wealthy queen invited King Solomon to her court to test the supposedly ever-present wisdom of the famous king. Presenting Solomon with two bouquets of flowers, she announced: "One bouquet of flowers was made by my very best artisans, the other is from the garden. We would like to see if you, in your wisdom, can tell us which is the real bouquet."

Solomon sat and carefully examined each bouquet. The color was the same, the leaves the same, both had drops of dew and, sure enough, even the

imperfections were the same. Solomon was unable to tell the difference. Just as he was about to admit defeat a bee flew through an open window. The people of the court tried to catch the bee but Solomon motioned for them to allow the bee to stay. The bee traveled around the room and finally lit on a bouquet. Triumphantly Solomon announced that that was the true, real bouquet.

What does the ancient story tell us? It tells us that even the wisest and most astute can learn from something else. We can learn from a blade of grass, a bumble bee, a butterfly, or a rainbow. All of these have something to teach us.

Nature is one of the greatest teachers and demonstrates a very special principle. It is constantly giving, constantly flowing.

The message today is to learn from nature. Do not take it for granted. Consider it important. God did not create things in order of importance. Everything is important. All creations have a function and a destiny to fulfill. Look to the bee and butterfly and listen to the wind. There is more for you to learn.

Commentary 50

EASTER

his is a special time of year. The restfulness of the winter season is past and a new awakening approaches. As we consider our attitude toward this day, we find that it is varied with emphasis usually on the temporary. Some are caught up in chocolate Easter bunnies, colored eggs, a new outfit, a new hat and food. All these are symbols, but behind these symbols there is an important meaning.

This is a period of rebirth. Look on the new green grass, the flowers unfolding, the trees budding. As things are occurring in nature, things are occurring within each person. There's budding, there's sprouting, there's a reaching out.

This is a time to appreciate life, your own Life, and how your life can touch other lives. This is a time to be concerned with Joy, a time to be concerned with Love. What is important is what the man who was crucified taught: an expression of Love. Are you loving? Do you love yourself, not with the ego, but with the power within, with an appreciation of the life unfolding in you? Are you giving? Are you sharing? Do you have and express love for others? These are the things to which we should turn our attention this season.

The world is growing and changing. You can see growth patterns, people gathering together, asking questions, entering the Stillness, coming into a period of Realization. This is an exciting time. Through growth comes change, and from change comes the new, an unveiling. All about you a new day is being born, a new time, and you are part of it.

Be concerned with what you can give to others. Don't be concerned with reward. It is important to give, to share, to reach forth. Share what you have, be it a smile, an embrace, or a thought and it shall

be multiplied over and over and over. From the larva will come the butterfly, the egg will become the bird. You will soar and you will enter into the Magnificence, into the Meaning behind the symbols. You will be at one with the bloom and splendor of New Life. Your Easter will take on a new meaning and significence. You will grow and change.

Commentary 51
MANY QUESTIONS: ONE ANSWER

We are living in a time of great speed. We are living in a time of many synthetics. We're living in a time when distance shrinks and takes on new implications. Yet, with all these synthetics, and all these "instants," there are some basics. They form a foundation and structure to feed when the synthetics would let us die.

We're living in a time when we have to say what is real and what is not. There are many illusions. There is only one truth. This truth has many ramifications, many implications, many applications, but it is there. There is one way. Not one roadway, but one way. There are many questions, only one answer. What is the essence of all beings? What is the essence of life? What is really Real? What isn't synthetic? There is only one thing, LOVE.

Commentary 52

COLORING LIFE

ecently, a lady came to me for consultation. As she walked through the door I was aware that she was all vogue on the outside but all vague on the inside. There are many people who fit that description. She had on false eyelashes and fashionably colored nail polish. She looked just right. Placing herself dramatically in the chair she took out a long cigarette and said, "You know, life has no meaning." I replied, "That's right, it doesn't." It nearly bowled her over.

LIFE ONLY HAS MEANING IF WE GIVE IT MEANING because we are life. It is the significance we give to it that creates purpose, that gives it beauty. Yet, if you were presented with a coloring book of life, and were told to color within the outlines, you would probably feel uncomfortable.

You would rather have pre-colored living, instant God. Most people want a set pattern of answers with glossy magazine pictures. They want to know that here are the good things, and on the next page, the bad ones. They feel comfortable with that format, but in essence, it is not a true picture. Things are as you make them, as you color them.

When I really enjoy something I want to share it with others. A few years ago it was the Grand Canyon. I looked at it at sunset and at dawn. I saw it during the day and at night. It was powerful. Sometimes I felt like an eagle ready to soar. I had a passion for the Grand Canyon and I took a friend of mine to see it. She took one look and said, "What a hell-hole!" I'm sure she had valid reasons for what she said for she was terrified by this chasm. Yet, it was difficult for me to see her viewpoint because to me it was a marvelous experience. I was a part of it.

MANY PEOPLE LOOK BUT FEW PEOPLE SEE, because to see you must experience, feel, relate to, become part of, unify. Looking at a rose and seeing a rose are two different things. In looking you're standing away from, observing. In seeing you are examining, feeling, becoming a part of it. And, in so

doing, you are examining yourself because as you become more aware, life takes on new color, new meaning.

The outline is there. It's your coloring book. Color it any way you want.

EPILOGUE

It is hoped that these words will create a spark within you. Now it's your turn to make it a bonfire.

Louis Gittner